W9-CIO-295

Can Rats Swim from Sewers into Toilets?

And Other Questions about Your Home

ALISON BEHNKE

ILLUSTRATIONS BY **COLIN W. THOMPSON**

LERNER PUBLICATIONS COMPANY

Minneapolis

Contents

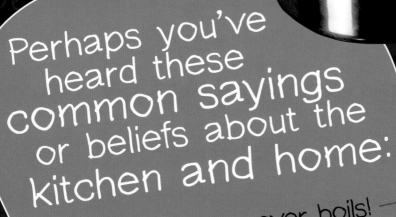

Perhaps you've heard these common sayings or beliefs about the kitchen and home:

A watched pot never boils! It's dangerous to talk on the phone during a thunderstorm!

But are these beliefs true? Is there anything to the stories you've heard? Come along with us as we explore beliefs about the kitchen and home. Find out whether the things we've all been told are

FACT OR FICTION!

Can a Ceiling Fan Chop Off Your Head?

NO—thank goodness!

Ceiling fans are in many homes. They're handy for cooling rooms. They can even help heat your house by moving hot air more evenly through rooms. But when fans are spinning at top speed, they can look a little scary!

Fortunately, ceiling fans aren't out to get you. They *can* go pretty fast. Their highest speed is usually a rate of about 160 revolutions per minute. But their motors are not very powerful. That means it doesn't take much strength to slow or stop the rotation. In addition, a ceiling fan's blades are not very sharp. They often have slightly rounded edges. They're also fairly thick—usually about 0.3 to 0.5 inches (7.6 to 12.7 millimeters) thick. That may not sound like much, but it's thick enough that it won't slice like the blade of a knife. Finally, household ceiling fans are usually not very heavy. Although some are made of metal, most fan blades are made of wood or plastic.

That's not to say a ceiling fan is completely safe. Getting in the way of one will probably leave you with a few bruises and maybe even some scrapes or cuts. But the average household fan simply doesn't have the power to chop off a head or even a hand. Industrial fans—which cool warehouses, factories, and other big spaces—are a different story. They're bigger, heavier, and faster. And while they still aren't likely to make you lose your head, they can definitely do a lot of damage. On the plus side, you'd have to be a giant to run into one!

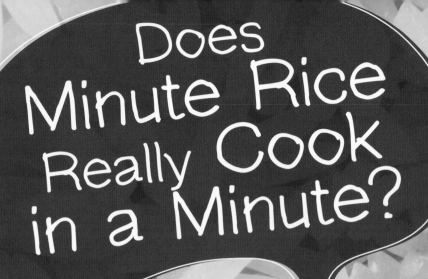

Does Minute Rice Really Cook in a Minute?

NOPE. In fact, it takes anywhere from about three to ten minutes to prepare so-called "Minute" Rice.

But Minute Rice, also called instant rice, does cook much faster than regular rice. Regular white rice takes about twenty minutes to prepare. That's because, by the time you buy instant rice at the grocery store, it has already been cooked. It's boiled in water and then dried out. When you put it in the pot, all you need to do is readd the water and heat it all up.

Using precooked rice saves big time in the kitchen. But instant rice also has drawbacks. For one thing, it's more expensive than uncooked rice. It also has less nutritional value. Most of rice's vitamins and nutrients are in the rice grain's outer layers. Some of these nutrients get rinsed away when the rice is precooked (though many instant rice makers do add some of these nutrients back).

Finally, instant rice is usually less flavorful than rice that you prepare from scratch. However, just as manufacturers readd nutrients to instant rice, many instant rice makers also add flavor. They use herbs and other ingredients to spice up their rice. But many cooks prefer to add their own flavorings.

All in all, traditionally prepared rice is the more healthful, flavorful, and affordable choice. But when you need your rice in a rush, instant is the way to go.

When you flush the toilet, tiny droplets of water are flung around the room. They can even float in the air for an hour or more after the flush. And some of those droplets contain some pretty nasty germs.

You obviously can't stop flushing the toilet. So what *can* you do? The simplest way to reduce the spray is to close the toilet lid before flushing. It won't prevent all the droplets from escaping. Some will still get through the gaps between the lid, the seat, and the bowl. But it will cut down on how many droplets spread around the room. You might also want to keep your toothbrush in a cabinet rather than on the sink. And you should definitely clean the bathroom regularly.

But the fact is, most people don't do all of these things. So why aren't more of us sick more often? One reason is that—surprisingly—the number of dangerous germs that spread this way is pretty low. We're exposed to just as many germs when we clean the kitchen sink or do laundry. Our bodies are also pretty good at resisting the germs that are common in our homes. After all, they've had lots of practice! Living with the same bacteria and germs every day has made our immune systems tough when it comes to fighting them.

If you're still a bit grossed out by the idea of toilet water splashing around your bathroom, here's a fact that might make you feel better—or worse. The toilet seat is often one of the cleanest parts of a house! Scientists have found that computer keyboards, kitchen sinks, and doorknobs are all, on average, germier than toilet seats.

Cleaning the bathroom is a nasty job—but regular cleaning can help stop the spread of germs.

Is It True That for Every Cockroach You See, There Are Hundreds More You Don't See?

NOT EXACTLY. There's not a definite number of unseen roaches for every roach you see. Estimates of lurking roaches for every one you spot include a few dozen, one hundred, three hundred, five hundred—and even one thousand. But it is a pretty safe bet that if you see one cockroach, there are a whole lot more in the general area.

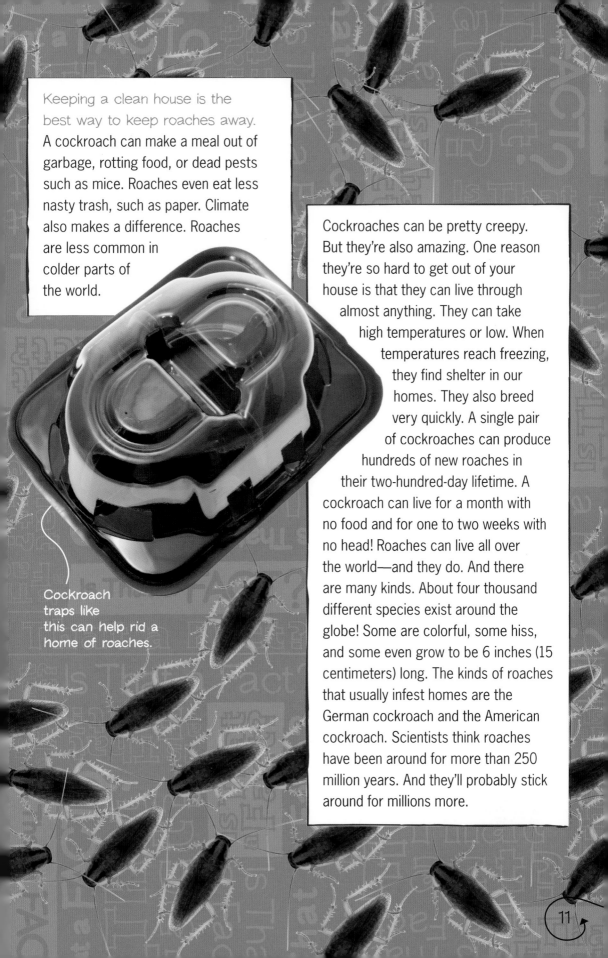

Keeping a clean house is the best way to keep roaches away. A cockroach can make a meal out of garbage, rotting food, or dead pests such as mice. Roaches even eat less nasty trash, such as paper. Climate also makes a difference. Roaches are less common in colder parts of the world.

Cockroach traps like this can help rid a home of roaches.

Cockroaches can be pretty creepy. But they're also amazing. One reason they're so hard to get out of your house is that they can live through almost anything. They can take high temperatures or low. When temperatures reach freezing, they find shelter in our homes. They also breed very quickly. A single pair of cockroaches can produce hundreds of new roaches in their two-hundred-day lifetime. A cockroach can live for a month with no food and for one to two weeks with no head! Roaches can live all over the world—and they do. And there are many kinds. About four thousand different species exist around the globe! Some are colorful, some hiss, and some even grow to be 6 inches (15 centimeters) long. The kinds of roaches that usually infest homes are the German cockroach and the American cockroach. Scientists think roaches have been around for more than 250 million years. And they'll probably stick around for millions more.

But even though they probably can, the more important question may be whether they actually do. There are hundreds of stories about various creatures popping up in toilets. Here are the facts.

Rats have definitely shown up in toilets. More than a few unlucky people have gotten the nasty shock of seeing wet rats in their toilet bowls. But just because rats have shown up in toilets doesn't mean they got there by swimming from the sewer. Rats do live in sewers. And they are very good swimmers. But toilet pipes are slippery. And if a toilet is on an upper floor of a house, the pipes are also steep. It would be tricky for a rat to climb up them.

Still, rats have been known to climb up some pretty steep inclines. If they really wanted to, they could probably scale the pipes. It just seems unlikely that all the rats that people have found in toilets over the years really went to all that trouble. So if rats aren't climbing into toilets through the pipes, then how—and why—are they getting there? Well, one idea is that rats get into most homes through holes in the walls. Then they climb into the toilet because they're looking for a drink. Lots of homeowners put out poison when they suspect their homes have rats. And poison makes rats thirsty. So if a rat has eaten poison, it would be even more likely to go into the toilet.

All in all, it's likely that at least some rats have arrived in toilets directly from the sewers, and many others have probably gotten there in other ways. But until someone develops a Rat Cam, it's nearly impossible to say exactly how any one rat ends up in any one toilet.

Is It Dangerous to Talk on the Telephone or Take a Shower during a Thunderstorm?

YES. Or at least, it's a little risky.

worry about. It's the lightning. A lightning strike can carry as many as 1 billion volts of electricity. That's a lot of energy—more than enough to be deadly. If lightning hits telephone wires or certain power lines, that current can travel through the phone lines. More than a few unlucky people over the years have felt that power right in the middle of a chat. For example, in 1985, two women in Denmark were having a phone conversation when lightning reached the telephone cable. Both had burns and temporary hearing loss. In 1998, a nine-year-old girl in Ohio had a similar experience. Other people haven't been as fortunate and have died.

OK. But what's so dangerous about a shower? Well, water is very good at conducting (carrying) electricity. In addition, water often travels through metal pipes—especially in older homes. Like water, metal is a good conductor. So if you're showering—or even doing dishes—when lightning strikes, the current can sometimes travel through the pipes and the water, right to you.

Fortunately, accidents don't happen as often as they used to. Modern homes and appliances have features that help protect us. But lightning strikes are powerful and unpredictable. Even modern safety measures can't prevent occasional mishaps. So to play it safe, avoid using landline phones during thunderstorms. And to be extra safe, you can even use thunderstorms as an excuse to get out of doing the dishes!

Stay off the landline during stormy weather.

Can Freezers Burn Your Food?

NOPE. Surprised?

You've probably heard of freezer burn. And it *is* a real occurrence. But the name's a bit confusing. Freezers can't burn your food in the way an oven can. After all, freezers are cold, not hot! But they can make your food get frosty and dry. And the name for this effect is freezer burn. Here's how it happens.

The air inside a freezer is usually dry. When food freezes, its moisture turns to ice. If air can get to food that isn't packaged tightly enough, the dryness causes the food's frozen moisture to evaporate. As it does, it forms ice crystals on the food's surface.

Freezer burn doesn't happen right away. Depending on the type of food, its packaging, and other factors, it can take from a few days to nearly a month.

Freezer-burned food isn't bad for you. But it is a lot less tasty. Freezer burn changes food's flavor, texture, and even its smell. Meat does especially poorly if it's in the freezer for too long.

The main way to prevent freezer burn is to keep the freezer's air away from the food. Try to package food as tightly as possible. Use plastic bags, sealable plastic containers, glass containers, or a combination of plastic wrap and aluminum foil. Keeping your freezer at a constant temperature helps protect your food from freezer burn too. So does making sure your freezer is never warmer than 0°F (–18°C).

A Really Cool Job

Before modern refrigerators, people used iceboxes to keep food cool. Iceboxes were cupboards or boxes with compartments for holding ice. Ice harvesters gathered ice for iceboxes during the winter. They carved huge blocks from frozen lakes and ponds. Ice harvesters stored their product in special icehouses all year-round. Then people called icemen delivered it to homes and businesses.

Do Air Fresheners Really Get Rid of Bad Smells?

NOPE. In most cases, they simply cover them up. Most plug-in air fresheners and deodorizing sprays have very strong smells. Even scented candles can be overwhelming. But these products don't really clear bad smells from the air. All they do is introduce new smells that overpower the icky smells you wanted to get rid of. Some deodorizers even have ingredients that slightly numb the nerves that help us smell. This temporary numbness makes it hard for you to detect any odors—good or bad.

One big problem with these deodorizers is that the sources of bad smells are still there. Those sources could include rotting food, garbage, or even a dead mouse hidden in some dark corner. Some odor sources can be dangerous sources of bacteria. So it's important to find these things and get rid of them— not just hide their smell.

Air fresheners also present another problem. Doctors believe that chemicals in some air-freshening sprays may cause (or worsen) asthma or other lung problems. Being around them once in a while is probably OK. But if you use them in your home every day, over time they might affect your breathing.

Odor Eater

Baking soda is a deodorizer that's an exception to the rule. Baking soda, or sodium bicarbonate, is pretty good at absorbing smells. Maybe you've seen an open box of baking soda in your fridge or freezer. Sprinkling baking soda at the bottom of a trash can or wastebasket can also help get rid of nasty odors.

ARM & HAMMER
THE STANDARD OF PURITY

Natural
Baking Soda
Cleans & Deodorizes

PURE, SAFE & NATURAL SINCE 1846
NET WT. 16 OZ.(1 LB.)

SAFE EFFECTIVE CLEANING USES See Back

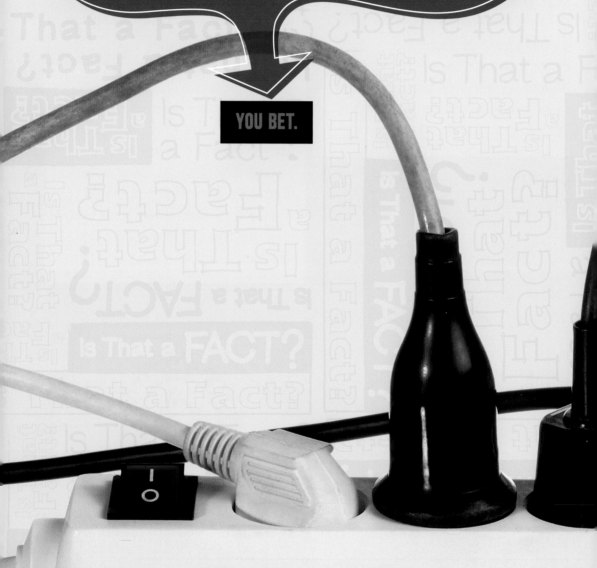

When Appliances Are Turned Off, Are They Still Using Electricity?

YOU BET.

Many appliances have a standby mode. The standby mode can be very handy for keeping track of various settings. But it also uses energy. Televisions, computers, coffeemakers, toasters, and other household appliances can all continue to use power when they are plugged in but not on. Sometimes it's just a clock or a light-up display that uses power. These use only a very small amount of energy. Over time, however, those small amounts add up. So if you want to save as much energy as possible, always unplug appliances when you are not using them.

You might have also heard that it saves energy to leave on lights and computers if you're going to be using them again soon. The idea is that turning them back on takes more power than leaving them on for a relatively short time. But in most cases, that's not true.

It is true that when you first turn on lights or many appliances, they usually need a burst of energy to start up. But the fact is that this first surge of power is usually quite small. In nearly all cases, it's simply not large enough that leaving the power on would save more energy.

Save Energy, Save the World!

If you want to save energy around the house, dozens of little tips and tools can help you out. Here are just a few:

Drying racks and clotheslines are great for drying clothes, and using them helps save energy.

- Wash clothes in cold water, and hang clothes on drying racks rather than using the dryer.
- Use fans instead of air-conditioning whenever you can.
- Turn heat down at night. Just cuddle up with a few extra blankets!
- When you're baking, don't open the oven any more often than you need to.
- If you do leave computers on, set them to go into sleep mode.

Is It True That a Watched Pot Never Boils?

NOPE. Pots aren't shy. They'll go ahead and boil whether you're watching or not! But this common expression has a grain of truth. Although watching the pot won't slow it down, it will probably make the process feel slower to you. The same thing happens when you watch a toaster as you're waiting for a bagel to pop up. But if you keep yourself busy with something else, it seems as if whatever you are waiting for happens a lot more quickly.

Boiling Over

You may know that water boils at 212°F (100°C). But did you know that this is true only under certain conditions? Water's boiling temperature can change depending on several things. For example, adding salt to water raises its boiling point. And if you happen to be cooking on top of a mountain, your water will boil at a lower temperature than it would at sea level.

However, you still might want to keep an eye on that pot. It isn't safe to leave the room when something's cooking on the stove. If a pot gets too hot and overflows, the overflowing liquid could burn someone. And liquid boiling in a microwave should be watched as well. That's because when you heat liquid in a microwave, it's possible for it to reach its boiling point without it ever boiling. This is called superheating. Superheated water can explode.

Check in on hot drinks when they're in the microwave. If they aren't boiling when you think they should be, don't touch them until they've had a chance to cool down. And before cooking anything in a microwave or on a stove, make sure you check with an adult.

Does a Dishwasher Use More Water Than Washing Dishes by Hand?

NO—not if you use it the right way, that is.

These days, however, dishwashers are much better for the environment. Most modern machines use both water and electricity efficiently. And the most efficient models use much less water and energy than the average human hand washer.

It used to be true that dishwashers used more water than washing dishes by hand did. Dishwashers first became common in household kitchens in the 1950s. They were advanced for the time. By modern standards, though, they were clunky, noisy, and inefficient. They used lots of water. They also used plenty of electricity.

Even with better machines, you can help modern dishwashers be as energy efficient as possible. One important tip is never to run a dishwasher that isn't full. If you have only a few cups and spoons, wash them by hand. Also, skip the step of rinsing dishes before putting them in the washer. In the past, many machines weren't good at getting off sticky or dried-on food. But these days, most can handle the job. Finally, don't run the drying cycle. It uses a lot of heat and therefore a lot of energy. The washer usually holds leftover heat from the washing cycle—and that heat (plus air and a little extra time) can get dishes pretty dry without using any extra energy.

Is It Dangerous to Stand in Front of a Running Microwave Oven?

NOPE. Experts agree that it's safe for humans to be near the average household microwave.

Microwave ovens cook food using—you guessed it—microwaves! These waves are a form of energy called radiation. We are exposed to different kinds of radiation all the time. For example, the sun produces a whole lot of it. But too much radiation can cause skin damage, cancer, and other health problems. So it makes sense to wonder whether microwave ovens might be dangerous.

Sheets of metal line the sides, the top, and the bottom of a microwave oven. This metal blocks the radiation and keeps it from escaping the oven. The door is a bit trickier. After all, cooks need to be able to see their food! They have to make sure it's not burning, boiling over, or blowing up. So the metal shield on the microwave door has very small holes punched in it. This design lets you look in and keep an eye on your food but doesn't let the radiation leak out.

Using sunblock can help protect against the sun's radiation.

Hot Chocolate

Microwaves' cooking power was discovered by accident. In the early 1940s, a scientist named Percy Spencer was walking through a lab where people were testing machines producing microwave radiation. Spencer happened to have a chocolate bar in his pocket. After standing near one of the machines, he noticed that the chocolate had melted. This messy accident got Spencer thinking. A few years later, the first microwave oven came out. It weighed in at 750 pounds (340 kilograms)!

Can Oil-Soaked Rags Burst into Flames in a Garage?

YES. When some types of oil oxidize (mix with oxygen), they release heat. As the temperature rises, the oil can eventually reach the temperature at which it catches fire. This reaction is especially likely when rags are in a container such as a bucket. The container traps most of the heat inside. Once the temperature is high enough, the rags can burst into flames, even though no match or spark is present. This kind of fire is called spontaneous combustion.

Garage fires can be very serious.

Up in Smoke

Oil isn't the only thing that can spontaneously combust. Haystacks also sometimes go up in flames. This happens when certain kinds of bacteria in the hay break down and release heat. Coal can suddenly catch fire too. That's because coal, like oil, creates heat when it oxidizes. And you might have heard of spontaneous human combustion— people suddenly bursting into flames. But don't worry too much about that. Many scientists don't believe spontaneous human combustion really exists.

Unsafely disposing of oily rags causes house and garage fires every year. Linseed oil is one of the most dangerous oils. Many people use it to treat wood furniture. But it catches fire very easily.

Fortunately, there are safe ways to throw away oily rags. You can always check with your local fire department for instructions. But a few common tips can help keep you safe. For example, firefighters recommend placing rags in a container with enough water to cover them completely. Another method is putting the rags in an airtight metal container. Fire needs oxygen. If air can't reach the rags, they can't burn.

Linseed oil catches fire easily.

Do Cast-Iron Pans Add Nutrients to Your Food?

YES. Cast-iron pans, pots, and skillets are just what they sound like. They are made of iron, a strong metal. Many cooks like these pans. They're long-lasting, distribute heat evenly, and can go right from the stove top to the oven. Cast-iron pans can also share a bit of their iron with your food. This process is especially common when you cook with acidic ingredients such as tomatoes or applesauce.

You might think the idea of a pan adding metal to your meal sounds pretty icky—or even dangerous. But in this case, it's actually a good thing. Iron isn't just a metal. It's also an important nutrient. Iron helps the body deliver oxygen to its organs. Many people—especially women—do not get enough iron in their diets. And that truly can be dangerous. If people get too little iron for too long, they can develop a condition called anemia. Anemia's symptoms include tiredness and trouble concentrating.

Special cookware isn't the only way to get your iron. It's in foods such as spinach, beef, lima beans, and nuts. But cast-iron pans are an easy way to pump a little extra iron into your diet.

Iron-rich foods

Bad News for Birds

Many people cook with Teflon-coated pans. Teflon is the brand name of a material called polytetrafluoroethylene (PTFE). This material has many uses. In the kitchen, it's used to keep food from sticking to pans. However, studies show that it is bad for some house pets. When PTFE gets very hot, it releases several chemicals in gas form. Breathing in these gases can cause lung problems. Scientists believe that humans would have to breathe in a lot of these chemicals to get sick—so cooking with Teflon isn't bad for people. But it can be deadly to pet birds such as parakeets and cockatiels.

Is a Full Refrigerator More Efficient Than an Empty One?

YEP. This fact might seem surprising at first. After all, you might think a fridge would have to work harder to cool lots of food than it would to cool a little food. And this is true when you first put in room-temperature food or warm food. But once the food is cool, the most energy-efficient plan is to keep the fridge fairly full.

That's because refrigerators lose their cool when you open the door. Warm air from outside the fridge comes in. If enough comes in, the fridge's air warms up. The food inside gets warmer too. Then the fridge has to work again to cool it down. But the more food a fridge holds, the less empty space there is inside. That means there's less space for warm air to sneak in and heat things up.

It is possible to overfill a fridge. If you pack way too much in there, the door will not close well. A tight seal on the fridge door is essential to energy efficiency. So go ahead and fill 'er up. Just make sure the door closes!

Make sure you know what you want from the refrigerator before you open the door. Standing with the fridge door open wastes a lot of energy.

Play It Cool

Another thing that can warm up a fridge is putting in leftovers while they are still warm. But you should do it anyway. That's because when foods made with meat or dairy products sit around at room temperature, harmful bacteria can begin to grow. So the faster you get your leftovers in the fridge, the less likely you are to get sick from spoiled food.

Is Betty Crocker a Real Person?

NO, MA'AM!

Images of the Betty Crocker character from 1936 to 1996

1936

1955

1965

1968

1972

1980

1986

199

The character of Betty Crocker appeared in 1921. She became the icon of the Washburn Crosby Company. This food-making company later became General Mills. At first Betty was just a name and a signature. General Mills used this signature to respond to letters asking for cooking advice. But by 1936, the company had created a picture to go with the name. Soon Betty's friendly face was on cookbook covers, coupons, and cooking products. That face has changed over the years. Artists update Betty's image to keep up with the times.

Characters like Betty are common in food marketing. For example, Aunt Jemima and Mrs. Butterworth are both pancake syrup mascots. But they aren't real women. And have you ever had a sip of Dr. Pepper? Well, don't expect any free medical advice from the doctor. No real person named Dr. Pepper exists.

But other famous food-related faces are (or were) real people. Chef Boyardee started out as Ettore Boiardi. He was an Italian immigrant who came to New York City in 1914, when he was sixteen years old. Boiardi became a successful chef. Later, he started a company making his popular spaghetti and other pasta dishes. Now his face and his name (changed to a more American spelling) appear on thousands of cans of premade pasta.

Uncle Ben, the icon of a brand of rice, is also a real person. So are Jimmy Dean, Mrs. Fields, Oscar Mayer, and ice cream makers Ben and Jerry.

Jerry Greenfield (left) and Bennett Cohen—the real guys behind Ben and Jerry's ice cream

That's Mrs. Crocker to You

Betty Crocker may not be real, but she's had one heck of a career. In 1945 *Fortune* magazine named her the second most popular woman in the United States—right after First Lady Eleanor Roosevelt. Beginning in the 1920s, there was a Betty Crocker radio show. A Betty Crocker television show first aired in the 1950s and lasted for more than twenty years. (Actresses played the part of Betty on the show.) There's even a street named after Betty Crocker in Golden Valley, Minnesota, the home of General Mills headquarters!

Does the Smell of a House Cat Scare Away Mice?

YEP. Here, kitty, kitty!

Mice and rats naturally fear the smell of cats. Or more precisely, they fear the smell of cat urine. This instinct helps them stay safe by keeping them away from dangerous, cat-filled areas. The instinct is so strong that some people use soiled kitty litter as an anti-rodent repellent.

There are some exceptions to the rule. For example, a parasite called *Toxoplasma gondii* sometimes infects rodents and actually makes them attracted to the smell of cats. This is good for the parasite, because it needs to find a cat host so it can reproduce. When a cat catches, kills, and eats a rat or mouse infected by the parasite, it also eats the parasite. Then the parasite can reproduce and survive.

These cases aren't the norm, though. In general, the odor of cat urine does drive away mice and rats. Of course, sometimes mice get desperate. Threats such as very cold weather, food shortages, and predators can drive mice into cat-inhabited houses. But when that happens, most house cats are happy to take the matter into their own paws!

Real CAT Smell

The Farmer's Furry Friend

The cat's usefulness in pest control has been famous for a very long time. About four thousand years ago, the ancient Egyptians began using cats to keep rats away from valuable stockpiles of grain.

Cats were important in ancient Egypt. This coffin of the Egyptian king Tutankhamen has a picture of a cat on it.

GLOSSARY

anemia: a medical condition caused by a lack of iron in a person's diet

asthma: a lung problem that makes it difficult for a person to breathe

bacteria: microscopic living things that exist all around you and inside you

conduct: to carry or allow to pass through. If something conducts electricity, it allows electricity to pass through it.

freezer burn: frosty, dry patches that develop on frozen foods as a result of surface evaporation

icebox: a cupboard or box with a compartment for holding ice. Iceboxes kept food cold before modern refrigeration.

immune system: the system that protects your body against disease and infection

iron: a strong metal that is also an important nutrient

microwave: a type of oven as well as a type of radiation that can be used for cooking food

nutrient: a healthful substance found in food

oxidize: to mix with oxygen

parasite: an animal or plant that gets its food by living on or inside another animal or plant

spontaneous combustion: the burning of a material without a spark or other clear external cause

superheat: to heat a liquid to a higher temperature than what it needs to boil

Teflon: the brand name of a material called polytetrafluoroethylene. Teflon is used to coat pans so that food does not stick to them.

volt: a unit for measuring the force of an electrical current

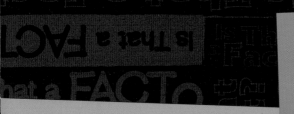

SELECTED BIBLIOGRAPHY

Adams, Cecil. *The Straight Dope: A Compendium of Human Knowledge.* New York: Ballantine Books, 1998.

Editors of Reader's Digest. *Extraordinary Uses for Ordinary Things.* Pleasantville, NY: Reader's Digest, 2005.

Marks, Susan. *Finding Betty Crocker: The Secret Life of America's First Lady of Food.* Minneapolis: University of Minnesota Press, 2007.

Mayo Foundation for Medical Education and Research. MayoClinic.com. 2009. http://www.mayoclinic.com (September 8, 2009).

McGee, Harold. *On Food and Cooking: The Science and Lore of the Kitchen.* New York: Scribner, 2004.

National Inventors Hall of Fame Foundation. 2009. http://www.invent.org (September 8, 2009).

Snodgrass, Mary Ellen. *Encyclopedia of Kitchen History.* New York: Fitzroy Dearborn, 2004.

This, Hervé. *Kitchen Mysteries: Revealing the Science of Cooking.* New York: Columbia University Press, 2007.

FURTHER READING

Donovan, Sandy. *Does an Apple a Day Keep the Doctor Away? And Other Questions about Your Health and Body.* Minneapolis: Lerner Publications Company, 2010. Learn whether some common sayings about your health and body are really true.

Everyday Mysteries http://www.loc.gov/rr/scitech/mysteries Check out this site to find the answers to some interesting questions about food, nutrition, inventions, and more.

How Stuff Works http://www.howstuffworks.com This site offers tons of information and answers to everyday questions, covering topics including food, the home, and health.

Kallen, Stuart A. *Urban Legends.* Farmington Hills, MI: Lucent Books, 2006. This in-depth book contains a wealth of information on urban legends—those well-known myths and stories about food, health, animals, celebrities, and other topics.

Miller, Jeanne. *Food Science.* Minneapolis: Lerner Publications Company, 2009. Learn more about food in the kitchen and beyond with this book about amazing food science discoveries.

Packard, Mary. *Mythbusters: Don't Try This at Home!* San Francisco: Jossey-Bass, 2006. Come along with Adam Savage and Jamie Hyneman—stars of the popular Discovery Channel show *Mythbusters*—as they try to separate fact from fiction.

Ross, Michael Elsohn. *Kitchen Lab.* Minneapolis: Millbrook Press, 2003. Want to turn your kitchen into a science lab? Try the experiments in this book using simple kitchen and household items.

INDEX

ACKNOWLEDGMENTS

The images in this book are used with the permission of:
© PetStockBoys/Alamy, p. 1; © Knorre/Dreamstime.com, pp.
2 (top), 10–11; © iStockphoto.com/Achim Prill, pp. 2 (bottom),
20–21; © Briancweed/Dreamstime.com, pp. 3, 30–31;
© Krneticv/Dreamstime.com, pp. 4, 23 (top); © Aderenyi/
Dreamstime.com, p. 5; © Rubyumans/Dreamstime
.com, p. 6; © Stocksnapper/Dreamstime.com, pp. 6–7; © Bjorn
Larsen/Alamy, pp. 8–9; © mediacolor's/Alamy, p. 9 (left);
© Newlight/Dreamstime.com, p. 9 (right); © Digifoto Green/
Alamy, p. 11; © Creasource/CORBIS, p. 12; © Ian Goodrick/
Alamy, pp. 14–15; © Gabe Palmer/Alamy, p. 15; © InsideOut
Pix/SuperStock, p. 16; © iStockphoto.com/Stockphoto4u,
pp. 18–19; © Gelpi/Dreamstime.com, p. 19 (top); © Peter
Arnold, Inc./Alamy, p. 19 (bottom); © iStockphoto.com/Maurice
van der Velden, p. 21; © Artizav/Dreamstime.com, pp. 22–23;
© realname/Glow Images, p. 23 (bottom); © Tihis/Dreamstime.
com, p. 24; © Fancy/Alamy, p. 25 (top); © SuperStock/
Getty Images, p. 25 (bottom); © Jupiterimages/Getty Images,
p. 26; © Alex Serge/Alamy, pp. 26–27; © iStockphoto.com/
Mark Swallow, p. 27; © andrew sadler/Alamy, p. 28; © Martin
Reed/Dreamstime.com, p. 29 (top); © Nicolas Leser/Glow
Images, p. 29 (bottom); © Food Features/Alamy, p. 31 (top);
© Kumikomurakamicampos/Dreamstime.com, p. 31 (bottom);
© Therry/Dreamstime.com, p. 32; © Redbaron/Dreamstime.
com, p. 33 (top); © iStockphoto.com/Spauln, p. 33 (bottom);
AP Photo/General Mills, p. 34; AP Photo/Toby Talbot, p. 35;
© Cammeraydave/Dreamstime.com, p. 36; © Verastuchelove/
Dreamstime.com, p. 37 (top). © J Marshall - Tribaleye Images/
Alamy, p. 37 (bottom).

Front Cover: © PetStockBoys/Alamy (left). © iStockphoto.com/
Glenda Powers (right).

Lerner Publications Company
A division of Lerner Publishing Group, Inc.
241 First Avenue North
Minneapolis, MN 55401 U.S.A.

Website address: www.lernerbooks.com

Library of Congress Cataloging-in-Publication Data

Behnke, Allison.
    Can rats swim from sewers into toilets? : and other
questions about your home / by Alison Behnke ; illustrated
by Colin W. Thompson.
        p.   cm. — (Is that a fact?)
    Includes bibliographical references and index.
    ISBN 978–0–7613–4914–3 (lib. bdg. : alk. paper)
    1. Housekeeping—Miscellanea—Juvenile literature.
2. Household pests—Miscellanea—Juvenile literature.
3. Curiosities and wonders—Juvenile literature. I. Title.
TX158.B54 2011
648—dc22   2009049496

Manufactured in the United States of America
1 – CG – 7/15/10